ROCKET FUEL FOR YOUR KITE

A Story of Hearing Loss and Hope.
A Guide to Ignite Weakness and Soar to Win.

JODI COSTA

Copyright © 2021 JODI COSTA
All Rights Reserved. Printed in the U.S.A.
Published by Two Penny Publishing
850 E Lime Street #266, Tarpon Springs, Florida 34688

No part of this publication may be reproduced, distributed, or transmitted in any form or by any means, including photocopying, recording, or other electronic or mechanical methods, without the prior written permission of the publisher, except in the case of brief quotations embodied in critical reviews and certain other noncommercial uses permitted by copyright law.

For permission requests and ordering information, email the publisher at:
info@twopennypublishing.com

Book Cover by: Adrian Traurig

ISBN: 978-1-950995-57-8

FIRST EDITION

For more information about this author or to book event appearance or media interview, please contact the author representative at:
info@twopennypublishing.com

Praises for
ROCKET FUEL FOR YOUR KITE

We all have struggles. Some are seen, while many are unseen. In this book, Jodi invites us into her struggle, limitations, and times of being misunderstood - into a brand new atmosphere of strength, living beyond, inner confidence and boldness through sharing her personal life story to inspire others. She shows, by example, that being brave enough to share our stories creates connection, empathy, and transformation to us individually and as a culture. This book is a message for every person no matter what they're facing physically, emotionally or mentally. The sky's the limit and it is time to soar!

CYNDA HARRIS, CLC
Founder of Grow Life, Inc.
Life & Leadership Coach | Speaker | Writer
www.growandflourish.com

My favorite line because it recognizes how far you've come: "I wasn't quite sure how to blend my disability into part of who I am. I perceived it as an end to the life I knew."

So much depth and exploration that you don't even realize it. While it seems that Jodi brings you a glimpse into her journey with disability you actually come out of the experience taking on personal transformation yourself.

MICHELLE HU, AU.D.
Pediatric Audiologist

Jodi bares her struggles and triumphs as she navigates life with an invisible disability. If you're facing challenges of any kind, this book will give you the tools to help you cope and find the courage to speak up. If your life is going remarkably well, this book will remind you of the importance of empathy and prepare you for whatever inevitable curve balls come your way.

CYNDI EDWARDS
Host of *StreetWise Live!*

for my mom and dad
who have taught me to reach higher

for my children,
Joshua, Jordan, Jackson, and Josie
reach a little higher than you think you can

CONTENTS

Introduction		7
Chapter 1	Kite Break	11
Chapter 2	Kite-ology	17
Chapter 3	Kite Doctor	27
Chapter 4	Kite Beasts	33
Chapter 5	Kite Aflame	41
Chapter 6	Kite Crash	49
Chapter 7	Kite Buddies	57
Chapter 8	Kite Blur	63
Chapter 9	Rocket Fuel Hunt	69
Chapter 10	Rocket Fuel Launching Pad	77
Chapter 11	Rocket Fuel Dare	87
Chapter 12	Rocket Fuel Leak	99
Chapter 13	Rocket Fueled Focus	107
Chapter 14	Launch	115
Contributors		125
Acknowledgments		131
About the Author		133

INTRODUCTION

Everyone is battling something.

HELLO.

Would you mind if we spent a little time chatting? You see, I have some matters to share with you. They are the kinds of thoughts that come from a vulnerable place. It's taken me a while, but I feel it's time to open up and offer some of my experiences, and the lessons I've learned.

From the outside view, this book could easily be labeled "a help book for people with disabilities." It's true. I have hearing loss. But, what has kept my fingers to the keyboard is not the disability itself, but rather viewing my hearing loss as a part of who I am from a positive perspective instead of looking at it as an end to happiness and a wonderful life.

I'll be honest, writing about my situation is helping me to start talking about it rather than tucking it aside and praying no one notices. My desire is that a light clicks on in your heart and we make an invisible human connection. And maybe my personal insight helps you travel life's journey a little more confidently and a lot less lonely.

I also want to hear from you. I prefer this not be a one sided conversation, which most books are. For that reason, I'm going to allow you some space to mull over the thoughts I share, to see if there is anything that appears in your mind that is worthy of jotting down.

Whether you struggle physically, mentally, emotionally, financially, or relationally, there are two ways your life can go. And the choice is yours to make. One magnificent thing I've learned throughout this journey of loss, acceptance and learning, is everyone is battling something. I wonder what your life is teaching you.

During my exploration of how to move forward with hearing loss, I became more aware of both the separation and unity that exists between body and soul.

*Though I have hearing loss,
it is only a portion of who I am.*

The title of my book reflects the relationship between the body you've been given and the soul you can grow. The "rocket fuel" represents your soul, determination, and guts. The "kite" represents your flesh and bones; your physical, earthly footprint of existence.

Kites are peaceful and go about their business of soaring gracefully in the wind with a lovely backdrop of brilliant blue sky and fluffy white clouds. Their structure is simple, but strong. Kites come in an array of colors and shapes and are quite fun. Usually, they are not flown in crazy thunderstorms or hurricanes (unless you're Benjamin Franklin). Nor could they withstand such aggressive weather. Or so we think.

Life is not a one-size-fits-all. Even though we are all human beings living on this planet together, we are not the same. Our paths are not the same. This book is sharing one way to consider how you look at yourself, your body, your talents, skills, and limitations.

What if you strapped a fuel tank onto your kite and aimed for the stars?

 What if you didn't hold back because of a weakness your life has granted you?

 What if, because of your weakness, you could soar further with grander purpose?

Let's fly a kite together and uncover wonderful truths about you, your grit and resilience, and all the amazing things you offer our world. Life can be a glorious blue sky of potential once you decide to hunt for the resources to fill your rocket fuel tank.

[chapter one]
KITE BREAK

The television was cranked up much louder, the *huh's* and *what's* were frequent, and it was more than selective hearing as my husband suggested. I learned my condition would most likely rob me of all my hearing at some unknown point. I was pregnant with my third child and it became undeniable that I was losing my hearing.

After testing, the doctor at *University of South Florida Medical Center* delivered the news that I have a degenerative condition called otosclerosis. It has to do with the smallest, lightest bone in our bodies. The amount of havoc the stapes bones can cause when they're broken still baffles me. The ear, the whole body, for goodness sake, is such a magnificent machine.

While the doctor was explaining ear anatomy, why I wasn't hearing, and what my future might look like, my mind drifted off in random and unexplainable directions.

Did I turn the coffee pot off?
Maybe I'll pick up Chinese food on the way home...
I wonder if this doctor has children.
Who chose this shade of drab beige for the walls? It's depressing.

How odd that I couldn't stay focused during this important conversation. I suppose my brain automatically shifted when the information was too intense to digest. Have you ever experienced a moment like that? I am most certain I had the same attention problem in eleventh grade biology.

I didn't have questions for the doctor. I didn't really have much of a response at all. A bit numb, I guess you could say. And also a twinge of relief, in a strange way, that what I was experiencing actually had a name.

When I was in third grade, I wanted to be Mary in the Christmas pageant. Two other girls, Sandy Simon and Tracey Starke, were also trying out for the part of Mary. I practiced my lines for two solid weeks. I nervously auditioned with Chad Banks, who was the only kid trying out for Joseph.

I remembered my lines, and in my 8 year old mind, nailed it. When the audition results were posted a few days later, I skittered over to see my name was not next to Mary. Sandy's was. My eyes scrolled down to Elizabeth, and there was Tracey's name. Don't tell me I'm a shepherd, or good grief, a barn animal!

But no. I was neither. Instead, my part was listed as *Unnamed Female*. Unnamed Female's role was to pack Mary and Joseph's leather bags on their donkey, which was actually two sawhorses covered with furry bathrobes.

It was a blow. I was humiliated and outraged. Someone got this wrong. I did everything right. I practiced, and was prepared for everything Mary would encounter in this reenactment of Christ's birth, including holding the real baby in the final scene. It wasn't fair and I didn't want to be the *Unnamed Female*.

When I was given my hearing loss diagnosis, I went through a similar response. I felt like I was handed the script for a role I wanted nothing to do with. I hadn't done anything to deserve this role. In fact, I had prepared for a much more spotlight-worthy existence.

Over the next several weeks after the "deaf bomb" was dropped, I felt like I was on a roller coaster blindfolded as I began to process the information of my diagnosis in unpredictable phases. I started realizing the weight of this loss. How something that I took for granted, specifically my hearing, was now something I thought about every waking moment, and sometimes while asleep.

Rationalization was my default emotion. Afterall, I wasn't in pain and I didn't look any different than before. I was relieved it was my hearing that was going and not a small list of other things I considered to be worse or fatal.

After I had rationalized the heck out of my diagnosis, *fear* crept in. How I was supposed to be a momma to three boys with hearing loss? How was I supposed to hear them cry in the night? What if they fell and hurt themselves, and I didn't know it? I feared being left out. I was afraid of being in total silence. I would actually get upset if the radio wasn't playing a song I wanted to hear. After all, I didn't want to waste my hearing on things that didn't interest me.

I was *confused* about whether I had done something to cause otosclerosis and if I could have avoided it. I read otosclerosis could be hereditary. Well, I must be starting a new trend for my lineage because no one in my family tree has had this condition. Another cause, according to what I read on the internet, is a surge of hormones, like during pregnancy. Well, gee. I didn't read that in the manual! As if gaining weight, morning sickness, and stretch marks weren't enough of a treat.

The worry monster camped out on my doorstep.

For the most part, trying to figure out my future mode as a deaf person was exhausting. I found myself thinking irrational things that had a million to one chance of ever happening. Yes, the downward spiral led me deep into the unrealistic depths of fear.

What the voices in the depths of fear have to say are always exaggerated and are usually lies.

Instead, I kept myself busy and tried not to think about the inevitability of it all. I had many things pulling at me for attention. Afterall, life doesn't take a pause for something like this. The bills still come, the responsibilities continue, and soon my parenting role in life would increase. There was plenty to keep my mind from plummeting into misery. Some of the most mundane, normal tasks helped level my mind because some things, like doing the dishes, would not change because of my hearing loss. Finding normalcy, helped scrape together my will to get creative and ultimately deflate the things that scared me.

But at night, when the lights were out, my babies were sleeping, and the world was still, I felt broken.

[chapter two]
KITE-OLOGY

Have you ever researched a car you considered purchasing, and during the process you suddenly see that car everywhere you go? I named my first born Joshua, because my husband and I agreed it was the perfect name for our perfect baby. What happened next was I noticed a kazillion other babies named Joshua.

Funny thing, actually not so funny, when I started losing my hearing, no one came out of the woodwork with their hearing loss story. My circle of people didn't have anything that resembled my condition. That fact made it quite difficult to blend into my environment. Often, I found myself alone or faking group conversation engagement because I couldn't keep up with what was being said. More than likely, I was sitting in a separate room bonding with the hundred-year-old over hearing aid woe's at a social event.

On the other side of that dreaded coin, I noticed deaf people more. But I wasn't in their group either. I didn't read lips well at this point or know sign language. My communication was incomplete with both hearing and D/deaf/hoh communities. On the hearing side, I felt isolated. On the deaf side, I hadn't yet learned the best way to communicate. Both sides provided guilt and loneliness in grand supply.

At gatherings, I would keep busy in the kitchen to avoid interactions. It felt safe and more comfortable than the awkwardness of having to explain my hearing loss. When I was caught in the situation of divulging my condition, it became an unpleasant topic that ended with people racking their minds for ways to contribute to the discussion. Usually, something like, "Oh, I can't hear well either. Too many concerts in the 80's," or "My aunt just had that surgery with the thing that sticks out of her head. Maybe you should try that."

I know now I should have appreciated their attempts to connect with me and used my inherent humor to lighten the mood. But at the time, I just felt like a misfit. All the places that used to feel comfortable and natural, now caused anxiety and isolation.

Without intention, I became a student of people. I observed since I couldn't hear. I stayed in the background and noticed people who were just as uncomfortable as me in a social setting. Without hearing a word, I saw healthy and unhealthy exchanges. My discernment level grew because I studied people. By removing this one integral element of communication, hearing, people's actions, facial expressions, and body language scream what words whisper.

People-watching was enlightening and helpful.

Now that I had captured the concept of seeking information visually versus audibly, I transitioned my studies to those with obvious disabilities. I watched as they maneuvered through the store with a cane or in a wheelchair. The man in my neighborhood that used a walker for his daily stroll and the blind gentleman who fares]d quite well in the church lobby. And sometimes, I crossed paths with someone who was deaf.

Watching people live their lives with struggles that some can only imagine helped me shape the vision of who I wanted to be. I saw some who were on the verge of rage. They were beaten down by life, bullies, and challenges beyond what they could shoulder alone.

I witnessed others who seemed to deal with their challenge by going about their business seemingly unphased by their circumstances. I would assume their mode or daily goal was to slide under the radar and not cause a ruckus.
Then, there are those who stand out from the crowd in the most inspiring ways. I saw them utilize their disability to actually improve their quality of life and make strides to positively impact

others. In other words, they found the rocket fuel for their kite.

The actor, Christopher Reeve, stands out in my mind. He was 26-years-old when he played *Superman* on the silver screen. In 1995, a horrifying accident left Reeve paralyzed and unable to breathe without a medical device. Though Reeve was a strong athlete, his body couldn't recover from this event. In a single moment, his bright acting career and other aspirations were altered.

He and his wife, Dana, became aware of thousands of others suffering with spinal cord injury. They did something amazing with their new, unfortunate situation. *The Christopher and Dana Reeve Foundation* was born out of this horrific accident. They became committed to finding a cure for spinal cord injury. I can not imagine that they would have started that mission had it not been for Mr. Reeve's accident.[1]

Out of all the cases I studied, Mr. Reeve's example resonated with my inner human the most.

---

1. www.christopherreeve.org/blog/daily-dose/a-single-centimeter-a-ruined-life-the-accident-that-caused-christopher-reeve-superman-to-go-from-a-star-to-legend

Whether the challenge you face is a direct result of your own actions, someone else's, by birth or a completely random occurrence, you have choices to make.

My future mode options seemed clear:

Easy Mode. Remain angry. Stay reactive. Put emotions on auto-pilot.

Mediocre Survival. Attempt to blend into the scene. Find a comfort zone.

Greatest effort. Greatest rewards. Fight through the obstacles until I soar to my potential.

I don't want to oversimplify the pain that comes from experiencing life's challenges. The pain you know needs no elaboration. At this point in your journey, you may already be fully aware your circumstance that holds you back is isolating, confusing, inconvenient, and scary. Your weakness separates you from what you consider normal. It is, at times, all-consuming and makes life feel extra complicated. If you let it, it can lead to the total derailment of all forward momentum.

> It's not okay to continually tug on the tiny string of your favorite sweater. Too quickly, you'll unravel it up to your neck. Understand this before there is a colorful pile of yarn at your feet. There are not enough YouTube videos to help you learn how to knit yourself back together. Before you pick at the string, tie it off the short string and snip off the end of self-doubt.

At this point in my life, after living a significant amount of years on this planet, I continue to grow more and more fond of this phrase:

> *Normal is Boring.*
> MARILYN MONROE

There remains a part of me who wants to blend in, and squeeze my life into a specific set of parameters to be accepted, to belong, or to be valuable. That feels safe. That seems comfortable. That appears normal. But it's not safe or comfortable at all, like wearing your shoes on the wrong feet, two sizes too small. And it's just my opinion, but I think "normal" is an illusion.

It wasn't until I decided to take a critical look at our culture's value system that I realized how limiting it is. Superficiality is valued. It lacks depth and refuses to see beyond the outside covering.

And there I was, trying to contort my challenges and personality, everything that makes me me, into the wrong sized stilettos.

I realized striving to be popular, thin, trendy, rich, or sexy does not provide the things I desire most. I'd much rather be excellent at being me, which feeds a healthy mindset and allows my differences to stand out in a way that nurtures my well being. And beyond that, keeping my talents, skills, and personality locked up in a box where no one else benefits for the sake of fitting in is unfair, and a waste of energy and mindspace.

I knew it would take work, but I decided to break out my metaphorical sewing machine and create a new kite. I've spent numerous, thoughtful moments figuring out what it would look like to strap on a rocket fuel tank and follow Superman's example. I don't have it all figured out, and I'm not sure I ever will. But the good news is, I am starting to recognize the reflection in the mirror, and I'm throwing away the too small stilettos.

YOUR TURN

 Think about the last time you studied someone who has a similar condition as you.

 Who is a positive role model you could study?

 What specialness do you have locked up in a box?

 What would it look like to release it and strap on a rocket fuel tank?

[chapter three]
KITE DOCTOR

Our first home was a little, white, ranch-style house with black shutters. It came with a lawn to mow and a mortgage to pay. The pride of ownership combined with a lack of extra cash led to a lot of DIY projects. I painted an old table and chair set that had been gifted to us back before painted furniture was a thing. Or maybe it was always a thing before social media said so.

The landscaper who was servicing the house next door offered to trim our massive date palm tree for $35. Not a bad deal, I suppose, if we had it. But that was quite a chunk of our grocery money. The date palm was the centerpiece of our understated front yard. If that palm looked healthy and manicured, our house looked happy. When it was overgrown, our home looked unfortunate.

As one of many do-it-myself projects, I climbed to the tippy top of the eight-foot wooden ladder with no fear. I carried the wooden-handled saw that belonged to my father when he was a boy, who passed it on to me when I was seven years old. We worked on many projects together. The garden shed was our best one.

Balancing on the top of the rickety ladder, I chose the dangling branch at closest reach. Two strokes of the saw into the overgrown palm frond and a giant date palm needle stabbed me through my finger. Clear through. My jaw was in an intense drop of disbelief. Yes, it hurt. But even more than that, I was in shock.

Holding my wrist with my hand straight up in the air, I scurried inside and loudly mumbled "I'm hurt." And the craziest thought kept flying through my brain: *If I can't afford to pay someone to trim my palm tree, I most certainly can't afford an emergency room bill.* It makes me laugh now to visualize what a scene that must have been.

With a brave face and wide-eyed children at my feet, I made my way to the bathroom to pour peroxide on it and instruct the most coherent child to find the tweezers. Are you wincing yet? I began to tug at the dagger but quickly realized the long end of the needle couldn't be pulled out because the other end had a barb on it. The barb end was too short to get a hold of with the tweezers. The needle was literally nailed into my finger.

At this point, I remained determined to remove the massive thorn. However, the more I tried to grip the barb with the tweezers, the further it dug into my finger. The needle was now more stuck than before. Geez.

I'm not sure, but I think I sat and watched a television show while trying to figure out how to remove it. I didn't want him to, but my husband went next door to see if Mark was home. He was an EMT and firefighter. He knew stuff! Mark came over with a little bag of tricks and started digging through it while he spoke to me as a nurse speaks to a child before they get a shot. A little sing-songy, which did not amuse me at all. He rubbed some numbing cream over both sides of the sword in my finger, and then we waited for it to take effect.

While we were waiting, Mark unknowingly explained that his cousin owned a landscaping company. Mark told us he was coming over the next day to cut his palm branches and he'd be happy to have the cousin cut ours too. I think the internal war I had with that information was a helpful distraction while Mark dug around and pulled the needle out of my finger.

I learned a lesson with that experience. I'm not saying I won't have to relearn it, but for now, I've embraced that no matter how determined and motivated I am to accomplish certain life goals, I can't pull it off without a little help.

As my hearing has deteriorated over the last twenty-ish years, I've been just as stubborn about asking for help as when there was a tree needle sticking out of my finger. Sometimes, it's served me well to grunt and fight my way through a situation in the name of coming out stronger on the other side. Other times, my obstinate and autonomous mindset has failed me. By that I mean, if I would have looked up around me and explored what options were available, possibly, I wouldn't have run myself through the wringer unnecessarily. What a waste of energy I've exerted on proving to myself that I should have just asked for help.

There have been countless group conversations where I've remained silent, nodding my head and matching facial expressions. The whole time, not understanding one word. Not even the topic. *Why didn't I speak up and request they slow down a bit? How come I didn't ask that they face me when speaking? Why didn't I ask them to repeat themselves?* This is a perfect example of what allowing my stubbornness to rule looks like. I think I believed at some point that I would catch up with the dialog, not have to say anything to my peers, and no one would be the wiser. This situation has never worked out well for me and is avoidable. I've never come across someone who wouldn't accommodate my needs when I asked politely.

I used to rack my brain trying to figure out how I was going to function in my later years. That thought always raced to helplessness, aloneness, and misery. Again, a waste of energy. Instead of doom and gloom, I've been keeping my eye on organizations, groups, companies, and individuals who provide services for people like me. They are everywhere. Some seem to fit my needs more than others.

> *Blessings can be missed when focusing on the pain.*

Deciding to not dwell on the needle in my finger and start looking around for help is what's been helping me most.

YOUR TURN

 What does your *stubborn* look like?

 How does it serve you?

 What are you keeping your eye on?

[chapter four]
KITE BEASTS

There are a few things that can send my happy-go-lucky mode into a downward spiral.

Overall, I have a good life. I have my moments of crankiness, but for the most part, I wake up believing it's going to be a good day. I dance while doing the dishes and sing in the shower. I do my best to shake off whatever threatens my upbeat mood.

My hearing aid battery is one thing that shakes my good mood upside down. When my hearing aid is low on power, there is a happy little chime that rings in my ear. I've come to hate that chime. I could be on my way to a restaurant to meet friends or in the middle of a conversation with a neighbor when that six-note song discharges. It's as intrusive as a tornado to a children's tea party. The chime reminds me that I have a disability when I've been working so hard to not feel disabled.

Another trigger is "never-mind." If you're hard of hearing, you already know what this is. "Never-mind" is delivered by someone when you ask them to repeat themselves because you didn't understand what they said the first time. When they respond with "never-mind," it triggers that "I'm not worth the effort" feeling. "Never-mind" says it's my fault for not paying attention the first time they said it. I know there are other reasons they would rightfully use that phrase, but to me, it's a nasty spark.

What do I do about these triggers? The battery chime is irritating, but as long as I'm prepared with a fresh battery, I can transition pretty well. To be honest, the "never-mind" knocks the air out of my lungs. It is a slap-in-the-face reminder of my failed hearing. It's embarrassing for someone to verbally pardon you from interaction without your choice. I usually sink back into myself and disappear mentally, physically, and emotionally. I have found marks on the palms of my hands from squeezing my fists so tight that they leave blood traces right under the surface of my skin. Those marks have held back tears in public settings. Internal words of comfort and strength are not available and I slither off from a public setting as quickly as possible with the goal of not causing a scene.

I felt like I let myself down for not advocating and I get mad at the person who rudely dismissed me. I try to shake off the negative emotions. I find it helpful to sit in my discomfort to sort through it all; a true internal processor.

Beyond all this, I realized what I find most challenging to shake off was the hostility towards my hearing loss. I have treated my disability as if it were a beast that was stronger than me and I felt like a victim to it's whim. Then, I act helpless and allow the beast to take over what I wanted to accomplish in life. It's a really unhealthy relationship. I avoided the beast and certainly did not welcome it into my world. In the process of this battle, I have put myself in harm's way a few times.

I'd like to share one vivid memory of a mundane task that became a turning point after I had my first set of hearing aids. As I was leaving the grocery store, pushing my cart out into the parking lot, my phone rang and I chose to answer. Why? I wanted to have the freedom to talk on the phone like everyone else, even in a parking lot. I've seen everyone else do it. However, I had to strain to hear the caller's voice which distracted me. I walked in front of a monster-style red pickup truck with an enormous shiney chrome grill. The Dodge Ram emblem stopped approximately 7 inches from my nose. The 'gentleman' reached his flannel shirt clad arm out the window, offered one finger while his mouth produced some colorful words in my direction.

As I sat in my car shaking, I decided there was a part of the hearing loss beast that might require more attention than I'd been giving. I had been shaking off the wrong part of my scenario. Instead of ditching the negative self-talk, I was belligerently shaking off the truth of my limitations. There are many things I can't do, like hearing people, crossing the street without doing a 360°, walk through a parking lot without paying attention with heightened sense, and know where the siren noise is coming from - or if it's actually a siren at all.

> *But I keep cruising, can't stop,*
> *won't stop moving*
> *It's like I got this music in my mind,*
> *sayin' it's gonna be alright*
> TAYLOR SWIFT

In the song 'Shake It Off,' Swift suggests that our best defense against negativity is to maintain a positive inner monologue, and allow positivity to guide our actions and experiences of the world. It's not a new concept by any means, but I respect her for calling it out. You shouldn't soak up negativity like gravy on a southern biscuit. You must practice dismissing toxic behaviors and self-talk.

By 'practice,' I mean, overcoming toxic self talk is not easy and it doesn't happen without intention. Beginning healthy internal conversations requires mindful repetition and patience with yourself. I've read various sources that suggest our private monologue contains as much as 80% negativity.

The first step to embracing my disability was becoming familiar with what hearing loss was to me and what it was not. Actually, you can replace the term *hearing loss* with whatever weakness or disability you're facing. Go ahead, fill in the blank:

The first part of embrace is becoming familiar with what _____ is and what it is not.

My turning point of embrace evolved after a few "in my face" reality checks that told me I can no longer ignore the beast. Specifically, a shiny red Dodge Ram.

Chew on these questions for a moment. You may have to dig deep. But, I encourage you to do it anyway.

YOUR TURN

 Who or what is your biggest beast?

 How do you fight your beast?

 What would it look like to embrace your beast?

 How would it make your life better if you stopped fighting the beast and learned to make it part of your life?

[chapter five]
KITE AFLAME

> *If you get up in the morning*
> *and think the future is going to be better,*
> *it is a bright day.*
> *Otherwise, it's not.*
> ELON MUSK

I had a lot of conversations with myself about how I wanted to deal with my diagnosis and gradual hearing loss. Early on after my diagnosis, I was in a season of life consumed by my young children, which included the normal household chores, church, and storytime at the library. Just as the doctors had explained, my hearing was slowly sliding down the scale.

My husband and I discussed hearing aids, but the affordable ones, like the ones advertised in the mailbox flyer, wouldn't do the trick. I would need high end hearing aids with powerful batteries and microphones, something just short of a radio tower coming out of my ears. That would cost thousands. Honestly, as important as hearing was, we didn't have the funds available. Until we could figure out how to afford hearing aids, I went without.

I was pregnant again and still had no hearing aids. Number four was due in a little over a month. My in-laws were treating the three boys to a day of swimming over at their house. This was a much needed break for me.

Just moments after I arrived to collect my kiddos, my father-in-law heard a loud noise like a gunshot. I didn't hear it .... well, you know why ... but when he alerted me, I made sure the boys were safe while he investigated the situation.

It wasn't a gunshot after all. My car was on fire and the heat from the flames caused one of my tires to explode. Yes, really. Tears rolled down my cheeks and onto my large belly shelf as three-foot flames billowed from the hood of my Isuzu Trooper. The firefighters pulled up and within a few minutes began to drench my burning car.

The boys thought the big, red fire truck was pretty exciting, but concern was written all over their faces, too. The Fire Chief explained that some electrical anomaly started the fire near the battery. The cause was never determined.

I'm not sure about you, but a car on fire in the driveway is not a normal occurrence for me. I was scared, and worried, and crying! Many "what if's" raced through my mind, which didn't calm my tears and sniffling one bit. We were already barely making ends meet on one income. With the car being totaled and another baby on the way, we would either have to buy a new car or I would be stuck at home with four kids and no transportation.

Even though the fire was now under control, my crying was not. The Fire Chief stood beside me and I'll never forget what he said to me at that moment.

"Why are you crying? This is a happy ending compared to the things I've seen."

That comment snapped me out of my melt down and into a perspective I hadn't thought of.

Yes, I would have to drive a rental.
Yes, we would have to find a car that accommodated two kids, two car seats, and two adults.
Yes, we're already broke and this was very inconvenient!

But good grief, girl! Think about what this was not.

This didn't happen on a busy highway with all three boys on a blistering hot June day in Florida. This didn't cause a fatality. This didn't even injure anyone. There was only minimal fire damage to my in-laws driveway, which was resolved with an insurance claim.

And finally, the best part of all. After we got a few bucks from the insurance company, we were able to buy a Suburban that fit our family far better than the Trooper ever could.

I realize not all traumatic situations finish this well. I honor this story in my life by allowing it to shape how I respond to life events of an unfortunate nature.

Here is how I process them now:

Let it out. Cry if I want to. Bottling it up is not helpful.

Breathe. Stop crying. Fix mascara. Dust myself off.

Process: assess, analyze, admit, and adjust.

Assess - take an inventory of each element of the situation.

Analyze - which elements need my attention and which ones can I remove from the solution equation.

Admit - what role did I play in this? Is this something I could have prevented? If so, how? If not, move on.

Adjust - reposition and move forward.

When I allow my emotions to take the steering wheel of an issue, moving forward is delayed and derailed. What I *feel* is my alert that something needs my attention. How I *respond* is not a job for my emotions.

Can we agree that life offers a surplus of surprises in all different flavors? There are various ways to deal with negative emotions and pain.

I was with my mom in the hospital recently. She had just broken her arm. She was in pain, but handled it better than any person I've ever seen. It was not only fractured, but also dislocated and they had to put the bones back in place for it to heal properly.

Honestly, it was hard to sit helpless watching her in pain and I couldn't do anything to fix it.

They were about to sedate her with an injection to reset the bones. I will never forget what the kind nurse instructed, "Don't hold your breath. Breathing through the pain is helpful to your mind and your body." The nurse demonstrated slow, intentional breaths while locking eyes with my mom. My mom's breathing slowed to match the nurse's breath pattern and she was able to climb on top of her discomfort.

Breathing techniques can calm fears, restore logical thought patterns, and bring pain to a bearable level. And the reverse is true as well: holding your breath intensifies the negative stimulus.

I've used breathing techniques to control my hearing related panic. In just a few short breaths, I remember I have hearing loss. And I'm going to be okay!

YOUR TURN

 What has caught you off-guard by going up in flames?

 How did you respond?

 Looking back, was that how you wanted to respond? If so, why? If not, how would you have rather responded?

[chapter six]
KITE CRASH

Before the COVID-19 pandemic, conversations with people sounded to me like they were talking through a thick mask. In some cases, hearing was so difficult that I could swear the voices were on the other side of a closed door and I had my ear pressed against it, straining to understand each word.

Because of the 2020 Coronavirus, masks were required in public places. It took a few experiments out in public for me to find out exactly what difficulties I'd face. With the addition of people now speaking through a mask on top of my "masked hearing", my limitations became exponentially multiplied.

When I'm out and about in a public area, people don't know I am unable to understand them. They may not even realize that I am unaware they are speaking at all.

Grocery workers are stressed out from working within the uncomfortable parameters mandated by the government and CDC. They find themselves in new roles of sanitizing carts and baskets, head counting to track how many people are in the store, trying to answer questions from a safe distance and dealing with stressed out shoppers looking for the toilet paper. Good Lord, the toilet paper!

While I plopped zucchini on the conveyor belt at the store, the director of bag options from the opposite end of the cash register would inquire about my preference. However, I have no idea what he is saying to me. By the time my cart contents are unloaded and I've reached the cash register, I could feel a strange tension. I said hello. The cashier responded by telling me that the bag person was asking me my bag preference but I ignored him. I felt bad and told them both I had hearing loss and I couldn't hear them. They didn't seem to flinch with this news. I felt like they had already written me off as smug or stupid. This scene was humiliating. I was embarrassed and more than that, it really crushed my spirit.

Later, I began to think of how many times this probably already happened but I didn't realize it.

> *Insanity is doing the same thing over and over again and expecting different results.*
> ALBERT EINSTEIN

I made a bold move to resolve this matter. I created a badge that read:

> *I have Hearing Loss*
> *Please write your message*
> *I'm not rude, just deaf*

And I brought a pad and pen as part of my experiment. It was very hard for me to pin that badge on my shirt for all to see. Announcing my invisible disability shoved a knot in my gut, almost more than being perceived as rude.

Here is the result of *The Badge Experiment*:

> I want to thank my dental hygienist, who happily wrote post-it notes for me.
> AND .... I want to thank the grocery cashier who waved hello and acknowledged my badge.
> AND ... I want to thank the guy at the sandwich shop who used pointing to ask if I wanted mayonnaise and mustard.
> AND ... the man at the pharmacy who gave me a high five through the plexiglass window after showing me that he was wearing a hearing aid, too.

I've had the most positive responses from hundreds of people. I posted about wearing my HOH badge on Instagram. Such wonderful people commented and "hearted" my post, supporting and becoming aware of how masks affect people with hearing loss. However, one person shared an adamantly contrasting viewpoint:

> ~~bxxh_l._rxxenxxld_scxxt~~
> From my experience, hearing people just dont care nor do they even wanna know. Most suck!
> To clarify, most of the hearing people i have come across and to tell them to repeat themselves as i am deaf, don't gaf and are nasty. I'm over them.

Clearly, this person was outraged and hurting. It made me sad. I wondered how this person was disclosing their hearing challenge. Were they informing or demanding? Did they give someone a chance to understand and learn, or did they write the other person off prematurely?

I thought about how to reply. I ended up typing this:

> I'm sorry for these bad experiences. Please realize that the "nasty" people might be going through their own invisible struggle. It's always a good idea to extend kindness and

empathy - no matter what side of the situation you're on. Praying you are blessed with kind people!!

I'm not sure if I wrote the right thing for her. But it was the right thing for me. Her reply:

> @jodi.costa then every single person who treats me like shit had a bad day. I'm glad you are so nice and forgiving- i'm not doing that anymore. If someone is nasty they will reep they're reward from me. You obviously havent had very bad experiences. Good luck with that.

Her response reminded me of the importance of notifying others of your disability or challenge. People don't know what they don't know. Speak up for yourself. Advocate for yourself. Get a badge. Wear a shirt explaining your challenge. There are organizations that support and assist with challenges of almost every type, and many groups (on social media and in person) that will brainstorm ideas with you. You may find a number of resources in your search. Choose what works best for you.

For me, the badge has been a success. While wearing it, I have confidence that I can handle situations that arise in a public setting. I've played around with different ways to word the badge and landed on the most helpful and impactful wording for me.

MY BADGE READS:

> I have HEARING LOSS
> Please write or text your message

The badge was so helpful, I started *The Badge Project*. I have donated badges to a few audiology offices to hand out to their patients who are struggling with their transition into deaf, hard of hearing, or hearing life. I've also mailed out badges all over the U.S. to people that I've met virtually through my social media posts. Looking for ways to help others has actually been a help to me.

Taking measures to alert others of your challenges might be the next step you need to take. And just so you know, there is a chance some people will oblige your needs. And there is a chance some people won't. And as my Instagram-poster said, they suck.

YOUR TURN

 What extra challenges have you faced because of COVID-19?

 What does self-advocacy look like to you?

 In what ways do you need to self-advocate?

[chapter seven]
KITE BUDDIES

Our families vacationed together; the Carlsons and the Bledsoes. It was the early 70's and we often ventured to the Oregon Coast; Lincoln City, Cannon Beach, or Seaside. I don't remember which beach it was on this particular holiday, but I clearly remember the childish anticipation of finally getting in the water. I may have been the inventor of *are we there yet?*

Our two, wood-paneled station wagons, tailgated the whole way there from our Portland homes. By the time we arrived at the stilted vacation home that sat 10-feet from the Pacific Coast sand, I was ready to bolt out of the car and marathon my way to the water.

Being only five years old, my parents put the kibosh on that. I was an obedient child, but this was pushing my limits. Brian, the oldest Bledsoe boy, interjected and offered to accompany me. My hero! Of course now, I understand walking a little girl to the ocean was a far better deal than helping unload the luggage and coolers. Nevertheless, I was grateful to my core.

Before taking off like a bat out of hell, or a kid out of a station wagon, Brian's mother warned me about the power of the waves. "Don't get in too deep. The tide will take you out with it."

The overcast sky made the wet air feel heavy. I could hear the loud waves crashing in the distance and the squawking seagulls overhead.

I ran and ran... and ran. From the edge of the sand to the water was a very long way. Sometimes as much as a mile. Such a vast difference from where I live now. The Gulf Coast beaches in Florida are a pretty short distance from the parking lot, to the sand and then to the water.

When I got tired of running, I stopped to roll up the pant legs of my purple OshKosh B'Gosh overalls. I knew Brian would catch up. I wished I had grabbed the buckets and shovels from the car. Digging a hole in the sand, a big hole, remained one of the simple pleasures in life.

The water was getting closer. I could taste it. Literally, the air was coated with salt. I remember looking back at Brian just before I reached the foamy rolls that washed back and forth. He was still strolling quite a distance behind me. I dipped my toe in to see how cold it was. *Oh boy, it was cold!* The salty suds covered my feet as the sand began to swallow them. I pulled them out and let them sink in again with the next wave that came up around my lower calves. And that was all it took. The power of that wave knocked my feet out from under me, and in an instant, I was under the icy water.

Arms flailing, eyes wide with surprise, the salty water captured me and held me tight as one of its own. I gasped for air when my head popped above the water for a split second. There wasn't enough air.

I have experienced this powerless feeling many times since this childhood vacation at the beach. The sinking feeling of being in over my head. The desperation of not knowing which way is up. And the panic of not being able to stand up under the situation, or see a way out.

Hearing loss spins me around repeatedly, and leaves me feeling disoriented, and wondering when I'm going to get my next breath of air. In reality, I need to reach out to one of the greatest earthly powers at my disposal. My friends.

Here's what my good friend, *Richard Hayes*, has to say about facing trials with the strength of supportive friends.

> Don't be silent about the frightening mountains you must climb in life. Be vulnerable and transparent to those who genuinely care about you and your whole well-being. Relying on others can produce unimaginable strength in your life, by adding tremendous value and fresh perspective to your situation. Let your friends support you and shock you with how they build you up and help you to move forward, which in turn gives you the energy to persevere! Please don't face challenges and trials alone. I've learned through personal life-threatening diseases & life-altering circumstances, that there are magnificent people that God puts in our path and for no self-serving reason they will climb the mountains with you, many times carrying you to the top, victorious!

Well, I swallowed half a belly full of saltwater before Brian yanked my tiny body out of the icy water by my overalls. Instantly I spewed and coughed up sea water from my mouth and nose. And a second later, my little body was fully enveloped in uncontrollable shivers. Brian's eyes were as big as mine. I trembled and cried as he carried me back to the house.

I've carried respect for the power of the ocean ever since. I easily equate the difficulties of hearing loss I've faced, with the strength of the ocean. This journey has spun me around until I didn't know which way was up. My hearing loss has revealed a lot about my character, resilience, and ability to adapt. And beyond that, I've learned life lessons and strengthened relationships. With my hearing weakness, I recognize I have choices to make: reach up when I'm drowning, reach for a helping hand, don't stop kicking, and watch for every opportunity to save someone else who's struggling. Because everyone needs a kite buddy.

And I'll always favor digging a hole over toe dipping in the icy ocean.

YOUR TURN

 What part of you is drowning right now?

 Who is your kite buddy or buddies?

 What are your choices?

 What kind of help do you need to ask for?

[chapter eight]
KITE BLUR

Personally, I think we get matters wrong most of the time. Especially how we view simple things that should be clearly understood. We overcomplicate, over think, over analyze things right in front of us until they become an unrecognizable blur. Each drawn out blurry pause results in lost time and energy. Staring at something hard without blinking causes everything to go out of focus.

Try it. Hold your hand in front of you at arm's length. Spread your fingers wide and focus on the sites behind your hand in between your fingers. Don't blink. And now, count your fingers.

How many fingers do you have?
Most people I know have five.

But with this exercise, you may have anywhere from five to ten fingers, or in some cases, all the fingers blur to an uncountable number.

Our vision fails us
when we focus on the wrong things.

Losing my hearing has made it difficult for me to focus on the real me. I never wanted to be known as the girl who can't hear; the deaf girl. Afterall, I wasn't the deaf girl for more than 30 years of my life. I worried that I would be labeled or written off as someone who I am not. My disappointment was magnified each time I wasn't able to hear something. And there I was ... fixated on my inability to hear. Focusing on who I was beyond the hearing loss disintegrated.

My hang-up with how I viewed my hearing loss actually made it a bigger deal than it was. I was wrapping up who I was, my worth, my abilities, my likability, and my existence around my hearing or lack of it.

Looking back, I understand why I had such a difficult time shaking off the negativity toward my inability to hear. I guess there was always a part of me that thought some miracle, magic pill would appear for me to take and my hearing would be restored. I remember one night I had a dream that I could hear again like before, and when I woke up, I was as mad as a smacked hornet. What an unfair dream to have, I thought.

Disappointment grew while my focus remained on my hearing loss. Such a small postage stamp sized view of the massive wall mural of my earthly presence.

One day, I was with my friend, Jennifer, and she introduced me to one of her friends, Tonya. She explained that Tonya is a wife, mother of three boys, homeschools them, does bookkeeping for a few companies, and makes the world's best chicken salad. Jennifer elaborated that Tonya grew succulents and was the best party-thrower.

When it was Jennifer's turn to introduce me, I held my breath. Jennifer went on to tell Tonya a bit about me. It was all true. It was all kind. And she didn't once mention my hearing.

Wait.

Hearing loss is not how others describe me. Why should it be the way I describe myself?

There is a lot more to me than my hearing. It's an inconvenience to me, but to others, it is just a part of who I am. And evidently, it's not that big of a deal. To them, I am worth whatever extra effort it requires to communicate with me.

It is true that my hearing loss is, at times, a colossal pain in the ass. It can be embarrassing. I'm pretty sure that everyone has something they're dealing with, whether it's social anxiety, stuttering, a limp, chronic pain, a lazy eye, or a sixth toe. These circumstances can be as large or as small as you enable them to be.

Why is it that we, yes, you and I, persist in tightly holding on to a self image that causes anxiety, worthlessness, or stirs up bad feelings towards ourselves? Could it be that releasing that perspective is tough because once we do, we'll actually have work to do? I mean, if I don't have a disability that is consuming my focus, I may have dreams and goals, fun and adventure, purpose and impact! Right?

While we both chew on that, let's go back to our exercise. Put your hand back up in front of you. Spread your fingers wide and stare at your hand. Blink. Count your fingers. Blink. Continue to focus on your hand. Can you see the details? I can.

I can see the lines on my hand show I am not afraid of hard work. I can see how my pinky curves like my dads did. I recognize my knuckles aren't as slim as they were when I was in high school. I remember these hands reaching for my new infants. I remember holding my mom's hand as my dad peacefully drifted to heaven. Even now, these hands type this book. These hands have cooked and cleaned, hugged and touched, worked and played. They are not perfect, model worthy hands, yet they are mine. I love the story they've lived and most assuredly, the story yet to live.

Blink.

[chapter nine]
ROCKET FUEL HUNT

> *Blindness separates people from things;*
> *deafness separates people from people.*
> HELEN KELLER

Hearing people have commented that total silence would be a dream. In concept, silence is peaceful and free. But that isn't reality when it's your life sentence. I've compared hearing loss to watching a movie through a peephole. No matter how hard you try, you'll never see the whole picture as it's happening. And besides that, I do not have silence. In addition to hearing loss, I have tinnitus. Tinnitus is a special concert of crickets that serenades me every waking and sleeping moment. The broken record that plays in my head is a high pitched ensemble of ringing, whistling, buzzing, and static, with a few dull notes. It overpowers most anything I try to hear, like standing next to a jet plane engine while trying to carry on a conversation. I call this the frosting on top of my crap cake. Why I haven't gone completely bat-shit crazy is a mystery to me.

To wrap up anyone's notion that deafness on any level is peaceful for me, they're wrong. The choice to pursue peace, no matter what you're going through, is your only true path to peace. And sometimes you must fight for your peace. I know the two words don't really go together. We don't live in a peaceful world.

> *Peace is not something that happens to you,*
> *it's something you nurture.*

Well, I couldn't seem to capture peace in the midst of the direction my life was spinning. I didn't sign up for this. Self pity seemed to be crouching under my pillow, in my back pocket, and in every raindrop . Oh, poor me. I had a big pity party. Party of one, actually. No one else was invited. And boy, I could *pity party* like it was 1999!

Without hearing, it's easy to feel isolated, left out, and alone. Watching people interact, laugh, cry, storytell... hearing only a word or two out of the hundreds that were spoken and never being able to keep up with a conversation.

A few years into my hearing decline, I'd had enough. I was tired of this deafness thing. I was sick of my circumstances, my story, my thoughts, and sick of myself. I was getting increasingly uncomfortable and just wanted to crawl out of this movie theatre and pick a different one.

It's hard to look at a flower that's losing its petals and find beauty. My attention is most frequently drawn to the blossom that has strong petals, rich in color. Those flowers offer symmetry and vivacious energy representing health, growth and beauty.

A few months ago, I was walking through a blackberry field not yet ready for picking. I noticed a lot of small green starts, some partially red, and only one or two black, plump berries. There were also lovely pink and white flowers blooming on the vines. Some were perfect. Others were wilted and looked like they were on their way out.

It occurred to me I prefer to look at the perfect pink flower or the juicy blackberry to see beauty; the bookends of their life. But the middle, the part where the flower wilts, petals fall off and the seeds are exposed, is not as pleasing to my eye. But one does not happen without the other.

My dear friend and licensed mental health counselor, Carol Burmood, enlightened me to her "in the meantime" concept.

It's what you do while you're in between situations. She gave me the example of turning in your midterm exam and waiting to see what grade you earned. Or having lab work done and waiting for the test results.

> What we do in the meantime matters, it's now this void, empty space waiting to get from here to there, waiting for our answers, our situations to change, our seasons to transition. Make the most of your meantime and it will actually help you when you reach the other side of your situation. God is in your meantime, wanting you to move towards him despite your circumstances and believe in what's on the other side of your meantime. When we lean towards His heart of what to do in the meantime, it's always better than we could imagine.
>
> - Carol Burmood

There is plenty to accomplish in between situations; take an online class, learn sign language, start a new sport or yoga; read a book, write a book or start a blog; visit residents of a nursing facility, plant a garden, sing in a choir, or learn to play the cello. There are many ways to be useful "in the meantime."

Out of desperation, I went to the coordinator at my church to discuss volunteering. I would have accepted just about anything he offered. I just crossed my fingers and prayed it wouldn't be cutting out paper stars and gluing glitter on popsicle sticks for preschoolers.

I explained the parameters of my hearing loss, and with a mad-professor twinkle in his eye, he said he had the perfect fit for me. He told me about the new guy on staff, in a new position with no one to help him launch his vision in our church. I didn't care who it was. I was just happy he didn't hide me away in the basement with one blinking fluorescent light, organizing dusty file cabinets.

As luck would have it, the new guy, Tom, ended up being a really great fit for my skills and interests. My contribution was designing a booklet to showcase the small groups in our church. Using my talents and creativity called on the part of me that had been buried under the weight of my hearing loss. I had almost forgotten I had those abilities.

Tom hired me a month after our initial project. Together, we shaped a new way to conduct our small group program. It didn't matter to him that I couldn't hear very well. Turns out, he deals with vision challenges. What a pair!

I attended a conference in South Carolina with my new team in the first year of employment at the church. I found out first-hand how ironic our respective disabilities were. Tom would take notes to share with me after workshops, and at restaurants I would read the fast food menu on the wall to him.

When you're tired of your current story but don't know what your next step should be, change your scenery and make yourself useful to someone else. There is a fresh perspective volunteering offers. Help is needed in countless places right around the corner from wherever you are. Your "in-the-meantime" can be an uplifting way to awaken your talents, and in my experience, it's one of the best cures for the downward spiral of self-pity.

I didn't know what outcome volunteering would bring, if any. It was truly a one dimensional thought that I acted on. To my surprise, it brought me much more than the effort I spent giving. Through volunteering, I found purpose, felt like I belonged, and discovered self-worth I had buried. It was the first time in my hearing loss life I truly felt a substantial source of rocket fuel. I was energized because I felt useful and not broken. Volunteering took my eye off the problem I couldn't change and I became a part of something much bigger than myself, my problems, and my abilities. And I didn't even get glitter in my hair!

YOUR TURN

 What part of your story tires you the most?

 Have you ever volunteered? Talk about that experience.

 Name 5 places where you would like to volunteer. What would you do there?

 CHALLENGE: Contact at least one volunteer opportunity this week. You might have to stick your excuses in a dusty file cabinet in the basement.

[chapter ten]

ROCKET FUEL LAUNCHING PAD

Medical devices aren't cheap. In some cases, they aren't affordable. I struggled with the feeling of becoming a financial burden to my family. It felt selfish to use the majority of the profit from the sale of our home on hearing aids instead of other family needs. With money, we could get a new couch, toddler beds for the two littles who had outgrown their cribs, light fixtures for the house, and a vacuum. The price tag of the aids were enormous, but fortunately, after waiting for three years from receiving my diagnosis, I was about to get hearing aids.

I fixated on spending the money, struggled with it, fought it, tried to rationalize that hearing aids were unnecessary. Then, I couldn't hear the conversation with my husband where he was telling me *Yes, it's a lot of money. But your hearing is taking you away from the family and having you back is worth far more than the price of the hearing aids*. Truth is, I hadn't placed hearing aids high on the list of my priorities. Mostly because my hearing loss was so gradual, it was hard for me to tell how diminished it was.

My hearing aid exploration began. It's amazing how many people, random people, become experts on a subject when you begin a new journey for a particular item. You could be searching for a carpet cleaner, real estate agent, hair salon, auto mechanic, or hearing aids. People, whether a relative, close friend, or stranger in the check out line, are positive that their recommendation is the best one and if you don't take their advice, you'll never resolve your carpet, transmission, or hearing issue.

With my head spinning off my shoulders from the overload of well-intended suggestions, I began going down the list of specialists to try. I could only bring myself to investigate two options. I selected one of the two specialists and went with it. I had absolutely no idea if I was selecting the right people to help me find the right devices.

I remember the sound booth testing with the beeps and words. But mostly, I remember when the audiologist placed the demo aids in my ears to let me hear what it would be like to have hearing again. And the promise of normalcy was in reach.

It was overwhelming. And strange. And wonderful.
It sounded like we were all in a tin can.
It was robotic and mechanical.
But I'd take it.

Once my new hearing aids arrived, there were adjustments and getting used to the new sounds, but overall, it was a success. I left the small office where they taught me how to access the bells and whistles available on these devices and told me I can call them if I had any questions.

And just like that, I could hear again.
Kind of.

The hearing aid set had a three to five year life expectancy. I held them together for year six. They were falling apart and my husband and I had yet to figure out how to pay for the next set. I was working at the church part time and putting money aside for a new set was a very slow process, especially with four young kiddos. My left aid actually crumbled in my ear and was unrepairable. Since my left ear is the strong one, I took the right aid and wore it backwards in my left ear. Awkward, uncomfortable and only partially effective. I didn't know how long I could go on like that, but even with the sores developing in my ear from the aid rubbing it raw, I was making do and refused to worry. Worry wouldn't put a new set of hearing aids in my hand, after all, and my husband was furiously scrapping together the money to make the big purchase.

I wore my one aid backwards for a little over a month, until a friend wanted to meet and ask some questions about my hearing. What started out as two friends having a conversation about my hearing situation, turned into a huge surprise for me. My friend revealed a brand new set of hearing aids were being paid for 100%. All I had to do was go pick them out. The kindness and generosity of this gift was mind-blowing and made my heart explode with gratitude. Within a few weeks, I had a brand new set of hearing aids.

I clearly remember picking them up from the audiologist. When he put them in my ears, I immediately heard everything clearly. Between the outdated hearing aids I was wearing and my declining hearing, I didn't realize how bad it had gotten.

I was elated all the way to my bones. But what happened next, I didn't anticipate. I left the office and noticed sounds I hadn't heard in years.

The sound of my shoes on the laminate floor.

> The ding of the elevator as I walked by it. It actually made me jump a bit.

The ring of the phone in the lobby startled me.

> The whooshing sound of the automated door caught me off guard. I didn't really even recognize the sound.

> The noise of traffic beyond the parking lot was a loud hum.

I got into my car and took a deep breath. My heart was racing and I felt anxious. This is ridiculous, I told myself. Why would these sounds send me into a frenzy?! I didn't remember this experience with my first set at all.

I started up the car. I heard the seatbelt chime. I heard the engine. I heard the gear shift into reverse. Another deep breath. I heard the acceleration of the engine as I pulled out of my parking space. I was about to turn into traffic and my turn signal just about sent me through the roof.

What the heck is wrong with me?!

I called my husband. I couldn't figure out how to work the phone with my new hearing aids. I sat at a red light in the turn lane, with a very concerned husband on the other end of the line while I had a melt down. Overwhelmed by all the noises, I froze at the red turn signal, which had now turned green. In a New York second, cars began to honk behind me. I was an absolute wreck! Luckily, I didn't get into a wreck. I pulled over and put my husband on speaker phone. He softly discussed the day, the weather, and our plans to go to the beach that weekend. I could feel myself calming. Within 10 minutes I was able to calm down, focus, and make the long drive home in rush hour traffic.

When I finally walked in the front door, my daughter, Josie, came to greet me. She simply said, "Hello momma." My heart melted while my eyes filled with tears. I had never heard her sweet little angel voice like this. The broken bones in my ears muffled everything to the point of not knowing what my own daughter truly sounded like. I spent the next two hours snuggling in bed with her and listening to her talk and sing to me. Josie kept looking at me to make sure I was okay and she'd say, "Do you want more, momma?" Of course, the answer was yes.

In the 1999 true-story film, *At First Sight,* the lead character, Virgil, is blind from a very early age. When he is an adult, his girlfriend urges him to opt for a surgery to repair his sight. But with sight comes intense disorientation and he is unable to interpret what he's seeing.

Days after receiving my new hearing aids, I remembered this movie. I felt a parallel connection with the main character, Virgil. Somehow it gave me peace that I was not a freak or losing my mind. There was simply a temporary disconnect from my ears to my brain. Realizing this reassured me that I would be okay and my brain would soon recognize sounds again.

One of my social media besties, Dr. Michelle Hu, gave me permission to share one of her brilliant posts:

> Not Black. Not White. Gray!
> If there's ONE thing from my heart to yours, know that hearing loss is NOT straight forward.
> It's so......GRAY.
> And individual.
>
> I might hear my mom but not my dad.
> I might hear you when we're in a restaurant
> but not in the car.
> I can hear you say the word "five" but not "six."
> I might "hear" you because I can see your lips
> but I can't when you turn around.
> I might understand a Midwest accent

but not a Texan one.
I might understand Spanish but not Italian.
I can hear one person with a mask on but not another.
I can hear you better in the morning
 but forget it in the evening.
I get tired listening to gossip but I'm energized
 listening to the passion in people's voices.
I can't pick up on sarcasm
 but I can hear your car's turn signal.
I can't recognize songs but I love music.
I can't hear the GPS voice
 but I can hear paper crinkling in the back.

My hearing loss may never make any sense to you, but it affects every single aspect, in and out, detail and breath of my entire LIFE.

It's just GRAY!

YOUR TURN

 Have you experienced something wonderful as a result of something seemingly terrible? Talk about that.

 Who do you reach out to when you get overwhelmed?

Is there something that levels your emotions when you've been caught off guard?

[chapter eleven]
ROCKET FUEL DARE

Have you ever watched an infomercial about a set of knives, or a hair removal system with a money-back guarantee for a better life? For only $49.99 plus exorbitant shipping and handling charges, all your wrinkles will disappear, and the cashier will card you for buying red wine.

My twenty-year-old self fell for a few of those hypes. But by my thirties, I had exhausted the pie-in-the-sky marketing approach. My jar of leg hair torture wax made its way to the trash can, along with my gullibility.

The pitch of normalcy was not true. It was a line delivered by the first hearing aid company I shopped. Looking back, that audiologist had more training in closing the deal than helping people with hearing loss. Their product did bring better hearing than what I had previously, but it didn't bring me back to pre-otosclerosis status that I understood them to describe.

I started seeing a new audiologist years later - let's call her Dr. Truth - from whom I got my third set of hearing aids and was told that pre-otosclerosis hearing would never return. Dr. Truth delivered this unexpected twist in my story and it pierced my hope. Thinking back to my first audiologist still brings up a distinct bitterness. Believing the lie (or uneducated proclamation) that my hearing problem would be resolved with better hearing aids made me feel foolish. I spent the previous eight years thinking that I might be doing something wrong or buying the wrong hearing aids.

After a lot of discussion and concentrated exploration of pros and cons, I opted to only get the left aid. My right ear had worsened dramatically and the very expensive aid would only help with sound direction. Hearing aids are expensive and although I have insurance to cover 90%, I still had a fat deductible to satisfy. The price wasn't worth the minimal advantage of having the right aid.

Over the years, many kind hearted people have asked me if I had considered cochlear implants. Honestly, I think I refused to consider it. I had become comfortable in my discomfort. It takes a lot of energy to explore new possibilities. I was certain I didn't have the emotional capital to investigate something that might not end up working, for one reason or another. Until I could muster the brain space and emotional capital to find out if there was a surgical procedure that could improve my hearing, I preferred to stay right where I was.

Change happens when the pain of staying the same is greater than the pain of change.
TONY ROBBINS

I was curious how my brand new aid would treat me outside of the controlled environment of the audiologists office. I was convinced I would be startled with the improvement; or that I may even tear up like on the videos you may have seen where patients are hearing for the first time.

It wasn't like that at all. Adapting to the new sound was not easy. The painful clanking of dishes at the dinner table was louder than anything else. Voices were either screechy loud or whispery quiet. The happy middle range was a rare occurrence, even with several setting alterations. I kept thinking it had to be the hearing aid, not me.

At my umpteenth audiologist visit, I brought brownies to the entire office staff for my constant intrusions. During that visit, the audiologist sat behind her desk and solemnly explained I had profound hearing loss, and my hearing aid would not bring me back to my expectations.

I nodded and I am pretty sure I thanked her before I left the office. I sat in the car a bit numb, almost like when I had heard the news that I was losing my hearing for the very first time. There may have been some tears and a chocolate milkshake on the ride home.

The time had come. The moment arrived where I was officially transitioning from moderate into profound hearing loss. The kind of hearing loss that doesn't hear an oven timer, a door bell, a smoke alarm, group laughter, the phone ring, a lawn mower, a car horn, a hurricane outside my window, a siren or an airplane in view. Let alone my daughter's sweet voice saying *I love you.*

I gave myself a little grace and a bit of space to chew on this bitter nugget.

What are my choices?

How do I want to handle this?

I didn't know. I felt trapped, like I was in my high waisted jeans and a crop top from 1983 and couldn't get out. Acting like the world was coming to an end wasn't a good option for me. Nor was dismissing it like it didn't matter. I was searching for the emotions and behaviors that adequately fit the moment.

I wish I could climb a tall ladder and walk a tightrope that hovered over the timeline of my life. I would be able to see the part of my life where I had hearing and oblivious that deafness would ever be a thing for me. I would look at all the times I took hearing for granted and chose to listen to the wrong voices. I would cherish the moments that I squared up and paid attention to the right ones. Especially those times when I listened to my dad's words, knowing that traveling along this timeline, there would be a day when the memories of his words would be all I had.

An uncontrollable smile would arise as I danced the wire over each child's first cry, first words, toddler conversations, and hearing them sing. Also our intimate conversations at bed time where they opened up and shared their heart with me.

I would shake a finger at the unimportant things I found important. And recognize the important things I considered unimportant. All of the life changing tragedies and triumphs would spike up off the line in vivid color.

I would hang on the moment I realized my hearing would

disintegrate. I'd stare at my scared, mad face, with tears waterfalling down my cheeks and my inability to form words to describe my emotions.

The tightrope perspective would make it easy to see those times I ventured off course and equally obvious where I took the crucial turn to avoid complete disaster. I would also like to tiptoe the rope to my future. *Will I make better choices? Will I listen even though I can't hear? Will I be okay?* All the questions that might be asked of a fortune teller or a Magic 8-Ball. *Better not tell you now.* Maybe I don't need to foresee what happens next. Perhaps, I just need to live it because I'm afraid of heights.

> *Progress is impossible without change,*
> *and those who cannot change their minds*
> *cannot change anything.*
> GEORGE BERNARD SHAW

I decided that I wanted to test how strong, resilient, and brave I could be. It was time to start cashing in on my emotional capital. I dug deep inside for scrappiness, and I found a curious student inside. The student seemed detached and didn't have much invested in my situation, yet she was eager to be my research lead. The first thing I found, while wearing my student cap, was several positive influencers on social media that posted smart, thought-provoking messages of hope. The student liked, commented, heart-ed, and followed.

To match her efforts, I fed myself scripture and prayed daily, some of which had no actual words. And then it started happening. I was scrolling along my morning fix of positivity on social media, and I saw an advertisement for a cochlear implant seminar. I sighed as I registered online to attend because the pain of staying the same was now greater than the fear of change.

While I waited a few weeks for the seminar, I didn't want to just twiddle my thumbs after taking a brave step forward. I began to post my struggles on social media.

It was like I dared myself to spin my kite in a better direction.

My posts were like mini journal entries. I confessed my hearing loss, exposed my cochlear implant journey, and shared the results of my consultation. For me, it was an unexpected magic potion that weakened the sting of not hearing and fueled my courage.

I shared both hope and disappointment. And because of those posts, I stumbled upon organizations, hearing loss/deaf institutes, and individuals who made large deposits in my courage tank.

I'll never forget the day I saw one of my posts featured on the social media account of a large hearing device corporation. It was my post about wearing my hearing loss badge and a glimpse of hearing loss life during a pandemic. Hundreds of "me too" comments turned into me sending out 44 badges to complete strangers with whom I had an invisible connection.

> *It was the second time I felt like all this self-work had resulted in a generous supply of rocket fuel.*

As I sit now, I still don't have a cochlear implant. I have entered my journey to CI with reluctant excitement. The bone conduction procedure (BAHA) would be good for me right now, but not a permanent solution because of my degenerative condition. It seemed my level of hearing loss sits right in the middle of technology qualifications. I still have too many functional nerves for a CI procedure. Not every patient gets all green lights. As is the case with me.

In limbo.

    In the middle.

        Waiting.

            Not yet.

                Sigh.

There is an impatient toddler inside that is screaming *I want to hear right now*. So, I choose to smile. I pray I will be able to move forward with cochlear implants one day.

My book will have an end, but my story won't.

YOUR TURN

 What possibilities are you bravely exploring?

 What brave baby steps are you taking towards a rocket fueled version of YOU?

When trying to land my first media job, I could have wallpapered my home with rejection letters. It only took one "yes" to change the course of my life. I haven't looked back and today I am grateful for many of those "no's." They fueled my determination to prove myself. Experiencing failure makes success that much sweeter.

CYNDI EDWARDS
Host of StreetWise Live!
Also known as a Host of the Nationally Syndicated TV show "Daytime"

[chapter twelve]
ROCKET FUEL LEAK

I know this to be true yet it takes me by surprise every time. The cycles of life don't stand still because I have this disability. The path of my reality is not paved with silky cotton balls that cushion everything from stubbed toes to nose dives. In all honesty, it feels like my road is spiked with nails and shards of glass making painful events of life that much more excruciating.

What I continue to learn is that there are many aspects of the world that can't be controlled; death, hardships, broken relationships, employment status, parenting troubles, and natural tragedies. But what I can keep in check is the discussions I have with myself.

Numerous times, I've been in heated conversations with myself as if a round table of individuals were gathered for a tea party in my head.

I've identified *Happy Head Hannah*. She dodges anything difficult and heads straight for the cotton candy side of life. Hannah is the first to serve up the warm scones and let everyone pick their favorite tea cup. She flits around making sure everything and everyone is happy. I appreciate her. But she takes a lot of naps.

Protector Pete doesn't wear a shirt. With his shapely biceps flexed, he wants to spit profanities and punch enemies in the snot box. He will not be picked on! I do love him, but often I have to put him in a corner with a protein shake.

Loner Larry insists on hiding under the table until everyone leaves. He keeps to himself and doesn't have much to say. His hobbies include poetry writing, sunsets, social media scrolling, and shopping on Amazon. He is most compatible with Hannah.

Then, there is *Billy the Bully*. He usually shows up late to the party, after everyone is settled in. He loves to disrupt the fun and peace. Billy typically starts by picking on our hearing and how no one has time to cater to our disability. Why would they? They have lives of their own. And we aren't really worth the effort.

Right before the entire party crumbles in despair, the theme song from *Back to the Future* blasts as *Realistic Rita* walks in wearing a psychedelic cape. She holds her head high as if she possesses magic sugar cubes for our tea.

Rita points to us all as she stands over the table and prepares to make her kazillionth declaration.

You! She points to each person.
You were created to soar.
You have a purpose.
You're not a mistake and you're not broken.

I sit with Rita for a spell and soak in the words I know to be true. I understand fear and doubt are part of our makeup, but I want to learn how to stick Billy in the trunk and not in the front seat.

My disability gets lonely and tiring. Most people don't know I struggle because I don't look different or wear a shirt that says "I have no idea what you said." I won't put my guard down. Billy will come back.

If I could ask you to do one thing for yourself, it would be to lower the crane hook and pull yourself out of the vicious circle of dreadful self talk. Then kick your legs like hell to swing across a great canyon and set down firmly in a safe place. Make sure it's grassy with cool breezes. Make sure it's far, far away from the toxic dump zone. Make sure it's sustainable and life-producing and bright with rainbows and possibilities. All for the sake of giving yourself a fair shake at soaring despite your weakness.

Be militantly on your own side. Cease the self-sabotaging monologue that diminishes your abilities because of your disability.

Say this. Believe this.

> *My joy and happiness aren't up for grabs.*
> *Not by circumstance.*
> *Not by loss.*
> *Not by words.*
> *Growing them is an inside job*
> *protected by me alone.*

While digging deep and dragging out the truth of who I am, I found a seed. It went something like this: I wasn't in control of what happened with my hearing, but I am in control of what happens now. That was the most pivotal conversation I had with myself. It was my "lightbulb" moment when I chose courage over self-pity, fear, and anger. And I began to let go of the expectations of what I thought my life should be or could be, and embraced who I am.

The man in a brand new sports car looked up and saw a helicopter fly over his convertible.

He said, "I wish I had that."

The man in an older truck looked over and saw the brand new convertible.

He said, "I wish I had that."

The man on a bike looked over and saw the older truck.

He said, "I wish I had that."

The man waiting for a bus looked over and saw the bike.

He said, "I wish I had that."

The man walking on the sidewalk looked over and saw the man on the bus.

He said, "I wish I could ride that."

The man upstairs in a wheelchair looked out of his window and saw a man walking on the sidewalk.

He said, "I wish I could do that."

The blind man sat on a park bench. Breathing.

He said, "This is nice."

Moving in and out of the territory of your weakness can be lonely, scary, and possibly maddening. But don't let that rob you from enjoying what you have, being you, and accomplishing what you were created for.

You are made up of so much more than your weaknesses.

I understand that the term "weakness" can mean a plethora of different things. It could be physical, mental, emotional, relational, financial, or environmental. You don't have to appear challenged to have challenges.

Who are you without hearing loss? Without the wheelchair? Without cancer? Without bankruptcy on your credit report? Without a criminal record? Without addiction? Without relationship failure? Without anxiety or depression? When you strip it all away, what makes you you?

Loyal	Patient	Content
Kind	Positive	Perfectionist
Generous	Optimistic	Bold
Creative	Realist	Deep Thinker
Spontaneous	Orderly	Productive
Funny	Faithful	Welcoming
Analytical	Confident	Persistent
Empathetic	Detailed	Persuasive
Adventurous	Inspiring	Resourceful
Sociable	Musical	Independent
Peaceful	Poetic	Tenacious
Competitive	Listener	Spirited
Determined	Friendly	Cheerful
Sensitive	Leader	Talkative

It's time to realize your body is merely a vehicle that carries your soul around this planet. Holding a magnifying glass to your insecurities guarantees you will miss all the good stuff. Despite your pain and exhaustion, you were created to more than survive. Your innate being is built to soar. Don't lose out on who you are and what you're meant to accomplish on this earth because your eyes are focused on what you do differently. Stop. Look beyond.

Take time to find the real you. That's *The Power of Love*.

YOUR TURN

 How do you talk to yourself?

 Would you ever speak to someone else that way?

 What is the next right step for you to start better dialog with yourself?

CHALLENGE: Try this now. Say two things that you adore about yourself. Self love starts right now!

[chapter thirteen]
ROCKET FUELED FOCUS

I would like to be remembered as someone who used whatever talent she had to do her work to the very best of her ability.
JUSTICE RUTH BADER GINSBERG
(1933-2020)

There was a couple that lived in a rough suburb of Washington DC, who fixed up bikes and gave them to at-risk youth, specifically boys. People would donate bikes that needed some work; new brakes, tires, or new handles. Often, the couple would teach the boys how to repair the bike that was going to be theirs. Many boys had never ridden a bike before, let alone owned one. Their bikes became a treasured possession and each kid took excellent care of his bike.

The group of bikers grew and it became difficult to find a safe place to ride together. They started taking their bikes to a wooded park, away from traffic and into nature. They rode in an open dune section where they would push their bikes to the top of the dunes and daredevil it back and forth all the way down. These boys that carried more emotional scars than many adults, got away for a while to act like children. Yelling, screaming, daring, clapping, and cheering each other on.

The couple found that the more they challenged the kids in their biking, the more seriously they took it. Biking went from a simple escape from terrible environments, to a way of bettering themselves and preparing for a brighter future. The group had become focused on discipline, self-respect, helping one another, and hard work.

The man found a trail in the park. It was narrow with low hanging branches. It wrapped around the far parameters of the dune area and off to the water plant on the outside of town.

The dips and twists seemed advanced for the boys, but when he asked if they wanted to try it, he couldn't hold them back. The man insisted on going first and taking it slow. Some parts of the path were on the edge of a drop. Other parts gnarled around tree roots and close to large, sharp boulders. The man led and the boys followed. Sometimes, the path was so dangerous they all got off their bikes and walked them to a safer section.

But they loved it and vowed to conquer the trail by being able to ride the entirety without stopping. The bike team practiced to increase their speed and agility. There were some scrapes and crashes, nothing major. But no one was able to finish the course without dismounting. Finally, the man realized what was holding them back. And he said to them:

> *"Don't focus on the steep drop to your
> right or the sharp rock to your left.
> Continually focus a few feet ahead of
> where you want your tire to go.
> Your hands will steer where your eye is focused."*

When I fully understood that my future relied on my ability to create it, I chose to concentrate my eyes on a few steps in front of me in the direction I wanted to be. I feel like I have accidentally stumbled upon successes simply by taking one tiny baby step in the direction where my eyes are aimed. Thoughts of unworthiness slip through the cracks every once in a while, but I've exercised my self worth muscles and can squash those thoughts fairly quickly.

I have a friend whom I admire very much. She bravely left a secure job that she liked for a passion that she believed in, loaded with uncertainty. She scraped up the courage to leave a teaching job and open an art studio for kids. Recently, I asked her how she talked to herself in order to make this happen.

> *I say to myself, why not me?*
> *I am smart, likable and tenacious!*
>
> LISA HELLMAN

And tenacious she is! In her new role as small business owner, she has leapt from the safety of teaching within the structure of public schools into a brilliant white canvas of opportunity. She empowers families in her community to focus on the therapeutic, skill-developing, confidence-building, creative outlet of multi-medium art. From comfort zone to impact zone. And it all happened because she kept her focus on what was her deeper, more unique calling.

I started journaling back in the early 90's. No ritual or routine, just random writings that I thought would help level my mindset and provide perspective. Brain dumping for clarity is a real thing. And a side note, I have a journal fixation. I own no less than 45 different journals. They each contain only a few entries. I have one that I found at a market while on vacation, another one I received as a gift, then all the holiday themed journals with clever sayings on the front, like, "My Favorite Color is October", and several more that I've collected over the years. It's a true problem. They are on bookshelves and in my nightstand drawer, in my sock drawer, the glove box of my car, every single beach bag I own, and even a few in my bathroom.

I found a formula I've used consistently in every journal. I use it to shed the negative, fear-based mindset that holds me back. I'd love for you to try it.

1. **Write the bad.** List the elements of my situation that have fear or negativity attached. Realistic and unrealistic. Record my fears. What is the worst thing that can happen?
2. **Write the good.** List the elements of my situation that have positivity attached. Humorous ones. Realistic and unrealistic. Let my imagination go free. What is the best thing that can happen?
3. **Who are the others?** Who do I know that has the same or similar condition, whether I know them personally, a fictitious character from a book, a T.V. show, a movie, or a celebrity.
4. **Resources.** Where can I get assistance? An organization? Do I need to learn something to accommodate this challenge? Is there a class or workshop that can help me adapt? A group to join?
5. **Go back to list #1.** Re-read.
    - Put a single line through the ridiculous fears that will

    most likely never happen.
   - Put a double line through items that are not in my control. Work on shaking them off.
   - Circle the ones that need my attention and are in my power to alter.
6. **Go back to #2 list.** Re-read.
   - Are there any more I can add?
   - Circle words and phrases that empower me or make me smile.
   - Underline the items that need effort to make a reality.

I notice when I take my eyes off my path, fear becomes my cement boots.

I am easily distracted by steep cliffs of failure, low, jagged branches of humiliation, and sharp, protruding rocks of mediocrity. Focus on the truth of what you were created to be.

> Don't let
> > your eyes
> > > wander from
> > > > your path.

YOUR TURN

 What path are you focusing on?

 Try the journaling formula I listed above.

[chapter fourteen]
LAUNCH

Have you ever flown a kite? I have. Mostly with my kids and husband in the park or at the beach. Watching it sail effortlessly across a blue backdrop is peaceful and mesmerizing.

The first time we tried to fly our rainbow colored, 3-ft. delta kite was not at all peaceful. Getting it off the ground seemed unattainable. It was as if the kite had a voodoo curse on it. The wind blew, we ran with the kite on a short leash and released it slowly, only for it to take a nosedive. To a bystander, it was probably amusing.

Eventually, after nearly destroying our kite, we found the sweet spot and learned the dynamics of wind and sail. The key to getting the kite airborn is to put your back to the wind. Then, holding the kite by the cross points, allow the wind to carry it upward. As the wind picks the kite up, continue releasing more and more string for it to soar higher and higher, keeping slight tension in the string.

Never have I ever seen a kite fly in the opposite direction of the wind.

Years ago, I escaped a part time job that I refer to as *the finance firm fiasco*. This job seemed perfect for me, being close to home and the hours my kids were in school. However, as I came to find out, hearing exact numbers in phone conversations was important to this financial agency. After several colossal errors, I resigned feeling humiliated and stupid.

I was determined to find employment that catered to my disability even though I had no idea what that would be. I started making a list of every possibility I could think of that didn't require hearing. I found many options:

Clean office buildings	Data entry
Factory assembly	Load trucks
Medical lab technician	Programmer
Lawncare	Auto repair
Web designer	Accountant/Bookkeeper

All of these were great options, except for one thing. None of them spoke to my talents and abilities. And even more than that, I wasn't passionate about any of them. I would be trying to fly my kite against the wind. Don't get me wrong, if my family's well being depended on it, I would do any of these jobs. Well, except the lab tech. I'm not fond of bodily fluids.

My job search was quickly becoming wearisome. I started thinking that my hearing would limit me to do jobs that provided money, but no gratification.

Eventually, I took a job at the church as I discussed in chapter nine. That lasted almost six wonderful years. Tom contacted me while I was between jobs after working with him at the church. He said a few mutual friends were inquiring about the three books we self-published when I worked with him at church. We white boarded out what it would look like to publish a few books. I thought back to when I was formatting, designing and coordinating his books to be published. It hit on several points of interest, as well as catered to my hearing disability. While designing a book, my hearing wasn't needed. My heart leapt, my soul was energized, and my mind was racing with creativity. I was in. This was it.

Tom and I were excited to partner with a few friends and get their books published using the experience we had built. We wrote up a little agreement, sent a little invoice, and bam, we had a little publishing company with four first time authors.

After we signed on our tenth author in the first 90 days of

opening our virtual doors, we knew we were onto something great. We expanded our team, wrote our internal processes, advanced our services, and dabbled in marketing. Two Penny Publishing was a real company - and still is today. We attracted an entire team loaded with talent: author coaches, ghostwriters, editors, proofers, cover designers, interior designers, photographers, formatters, marketing coaches, audiobook production, and ebook formatters.

I can't say that every step of my publishing journey has been smooth sailing. As a matter of fact, my publishing kite has crashed and burned more than once. The difference is, I am passionate about helping people see their dream of becoming a published author come to life. And I'm willing to fail, and learn, and stretch, and continually grow to become better and better.

What I've learned most from flying my publishing kite is this;

My disability can't erase my abilities.

And, without my hearing loss condition, I may have never landed this role as CEO at a company that I am privileged to pour my heart, soul, and creativity into.

I am
alive
needed
talented
hearing impaired
blessed!

LAST THOUGHTS.

November 2001, I was traveling with my nine month old baby to visit my sister for Thanksgiving. It was right after 9/11 and the air travel scene was intense. We scheduled this trip far before the national disaster and didn't want to cancel our plans. My sister and I both agreed it was probably the safest time to travel.

There was a chill in the air as I stood outside before the sun rose. I was waiting in line with my baby wrapped in my arms, dragging my suitcase, carry on, diaper bag, and pack-n-play to the first of several checkpoints. The lack of chatter was eerie since I was surrounded by hundreds of people.

Military SWAT-looking guards with rifles and bullet-proof vests patrolled the area. It was intimidating. I watched one guard walk up to a man, and without a word, pulled his backpack open with it still on his back. He rummaged through for about 10 seconds, then moved on. I had absolutely nothing to hide, but I was nervous and uncomfortable.

The line started moving forward. I bent down to grab one of the bags, and shove the rest along with my foot, when I spotted one of the guards headed my way. *Was there someone in question near me? Was I in danger?* I was wrong, he was headed straight toward me.

Without a word, he reached down in front of me, picked up all of my luggage, and instructed me to follow him. Clinging to my baby, I shuffled my feet quickly behind him, watching one of his weapons bouncing on his back as he walked. He escorted me inside, and directly to the front of the line at the ticket counter. After he put my bags on a cart and walked away, I quietly hollered after him a soft "thank you." As quick as that, my load was lightened, my journey was shortened, and I was at the front of the line.

There will be turbulent winds and scary thunderstorms in your journey. Most likely, you're riding in bad weather of some type right now. There will be pain, challenges, and tasks that seem impossible. You may even ask the question "Why me?" in a voice of frustration and defeat. I will not lie and say that once you decide to feed more fuel to your abilities than your disability, that your kite will soar to new heights with the greatest of ease. I am saying that each step you take moves you, all of you, to a stronger, more powerful position to flex through violent hurricanes and terrifying squalls. And it's worth the effort.

Just like the stapes bone, the smallest and lightest circumstance can cause a significant redirection in your life. I hope you use every ounce of energy to fuel that opportunity to help you win.

> *Life is not a journey to the grave with the intention of arriving safely in a well preserved body, but rather to skid in broadside, thoroughly used up, totally worn out, and loudly proclaiming,*
> *"Wow what a ride!"*
>
> HUNTER S. THOMPSON,
> *The Proud Highway: Saga of a Desperate Southern Gentleman,*
> *1955-1967*

YOUR TURN

 What will your rocket fuel be?

- Volunteer?
- Learn more about your condition?
- Find an organization that can help?
- Do you need education?
- Ask for help?
- Start up your own group?

Plan it out:

[thank you]
CONTRIBUTORS

CAROL BURMOOD, LMHC

Carol is the founder of *Life Impact Counseling* where she has provided years of Life Coaching and Counseling to those in search of healing and personal growth. With over 20 years of experience she has a unique style of combining faith and 'living with intention strategies' to achieve your purpose-driven goals and dreams.

Recently, she co-authored her second book titled, *You Are Here*, that takes the reader through a process of uncovering their authentic self and establishing a healthy mindset and goals to build the life they were created to live and love!

Carol also co-authored *MentorUS*, a book designed to walk couples through premarital counseling for the church community and has led various personal growth groups and mentoring. Carol lives in Florida with her husband, Dean of 23 years and daughter, son-in-law, and 3 amazing grandchildren.

She is currently working on the *You Are Here* project for 2022 to include e-groups and teaching events. For more go to Lifeimpactcoaching.us

CYNDI EDWARDS

Cyndi is a journalist who hosted morning TV shows for almost 25 years. She currently hosts *Streetwise Live!* which features public companies looking to share their latest news.

When they're not at home spoiling their golden doodle, Cyndi and her husband Colin can be found volunteering or exploring the great outdoors.

Find *Streetwise Live!* on YouTube.

RICHARD W. HAYES

Richard is the Chief Executive Officer and managing partner of *Digital Lightbridge®* (dlb.marketing). Hayes founded the creative digital agency in early 2001, and remains faithful to its mission of helping companies achieve their business objectives through strategic marketing solutions. Rich has over 30 years of diverse experience in advertising and marketing, having previously held executive positions with Fortune 500 companies and several major communications businesses.

Rich is a survivor of stage IVc "terminal" head and neck cancer. He was diagnosed in early 2010, and miraculously remains incredibly healthy and 100% cancer-free. Hayes is active in his community, currently serving on the boards of several Christian ministries and vital nonprofit agencies.

Rich and his exquisite wife, Nikki, live in Dade City (North Tampa Bay, Florida). They are the proud parents of five, way-above-average, children (Chandler, Mitchell, Hunter, Tristan, and Isabella)

Fun Facts: Rich served for five years as a volunteer firefighter and he portrayed a CPI (Child Protection Investigator) in the Gasparilla International Film Festival award-winning film Pharmboy.

MICHELLE HU, AU.D.

Dr. Hu is the creator of the @Mama.Hu.Hears community on Instagram (Mama Hu Hears community group on Facebook), an account inspired by her own patients growing up, having children of their own and asking Michelle how she has coped with and managed different real-life situations such as movie theaters, group conversations and motherhood. Michelle grew up with a progressive hearing loss and has worn hearing aids since the age of 3 years. She now has bilateral cochlear implants.

Michelle joined the audiology team at Rady Children's Hospital San Diego in 2009, following completion of her doctorate of audiology from the Northeast Ohio Audiology Consortium at the University of Akron. She graduated from Case Western Reserve University in Cleveland with a Bachelor of Arts in sociology and chemistry in 2005. Michelle is part of the Cochlear Implant and Hearing Aid Management teams. She is a fellow of the American Academy of Audiology and holds a Certificate of Clinical Competence from the American Speech-Language-Hearing Association.

My Father
RON CARLSON
March 1935 - August 2017

You modeled kindness, selflessness, and excellence.
You were an amazing writer who donated your talents
to churches and missionary organizations.
More than all of that, you were my dad.
The best dad ever.

[thank you]
ACKNOWLEDGMENTS

Mary Brazelton, Lorrie Shepard, and Lindi Shepard - My super smart and skilled family members who generously gave their time and expertise to read, edit, and suggest through those first *rough* drafts. Your input and perspective has proven to be invaluable.

John Costa - Thank you for encouraging me to not hold back. Your book is next!

Tom, Holly, Karen, Jessica - My team. You all have held me to a high standard and pushed me to be a better writer and storyteller. You all possess such great talent and I'm honored to work with you at Two Penny Publishing.

Adrian Traurig - You nailed it. I love the cover of my book. It relays all the hope and joy I want to share with each reader. Thank you!

Jen McCoy, Lisa Miller, and Kim McLeod - Friends forever. When I said I was going to write a book, you didn't look at me like I was crazy. I heard from one of you that I would be crazy not to. Thank you for the reassurance and cheering me on to *the end*.

Carol Burmood - I have so much respect for you and all the good work you provide to hurting and confused hearts. I'm grateful you've allowed me to share your concept with my readers. *In the meantime* has saved me many times before. I expect it will bring success to me in the future as well.

Janna Cowper - The feedback you provided after reading my manuscript was a blessing. I respect your insight and am grateful for your willingness to help make a better version of my story. I still occassionaly shake my head at how lucky I am to have connected with you on social media. I know we have more projects to partner on together.

Michelle Hu - I have many nick-names for you. *Wonder Woman, Hu's Awesome?!* My discomfort and confusion with my hearing loss led to a desperate move of becoming vulnerable on social media. Finding you has reminded me that there are many wonderful blessings just outside my normal reach. Knowing you has helped me shape a healthier mindset toward my disability. Thank you, Michelle.

Richard Hayes, Lisa Hellman, Cynda Harris, and Cyndi Edwards - Thank you for believeing in me and supporting me in sharing my story. I appreciate the way you jumped in feet first to be a part of this venture. It is definitely a better book because of your contributions.

[me]
ABOUT THE AUTHOR

Jodi Costa is an Oregonian, Portland style. However, she moved to Florida with her parents at the age of 15, and that's where she stayed put.

Jodi's later-in-life hearing loss was unexpected, yet she considers it one of the most pivotal events of her life. She found determination and grit through her disability, which has led to purpose and opportunities.

Jodi is the Chief Executive Officer of Two Penny Publishing, a growing partnership publishing company she co-founded with Tom Goodlet. The brave step of starting a new company is one of the most impactful life-changing blessings she may never have encountered had it not been for her hearing loss.

Made in United States
Orlando, FL
03 December 2021